Below the Brightness

This is poetry of the highest order. Metrically and musically deft and finely wrought, it is full of the sensitivity to sound and meaning, close observation, nascent metaphor, and surprising revelation that we look for in the best poetry. The sheer variety of forms and themes on display here, and Searcy's mastery of both form and theme is all the more remarkable for a first collection. I have found my appreciation of both life and faith deepened and informed by these poems.
—**Malcolm Guite**, author and editor of *The Word in the Wilderness*

Steven Searcy's spare, controlled poems evoke a rich cosmos in which control—our control over things, at any rate—is always tenuous. Tracing the arc of the seasons, in worlds both natural and domestic, in the ravages of weather and time and in small rituals of daily life and prayer, this debut collection acknowledges the frailty of a fallen creation still, mysteriously, indwelt and held together by its creator. These are poems which both mark beauty, in all its large and small material occurrences, and long for it, knowing that the beauty we observe before us is not all there is: "everything living moves and weaves and strives / because love moves, and the Lord of love lives."
—**Sally Thomas**, author of *Motherland*

Searcy is the George Herbert of the Atlanta suburbs, but what keeps him from being a mere imitator is his formal innovation. He is, in particular, a master of the short line, which adds a freshness and spontaneity to his own spiritual reflections. Highly recommended.
—**Burl Horniachek**, editor of *To Heaven's Rim: The Kingdom Poets Book of World Christian Poetry*

Reverent and reflective, penitent and penetrating, humble and hopeful: these are words that come to mind as I read this beautiful collection of poems by Steven Searcy. You will be blessed—challenged and comforted—as you meditate on each entry.
—**Matthew Y. Emerson**, Co-Provost & Academic Dean, Oklahoma Baptist University

In these pages and poems, Steven's vivid word pictures draw me into the realities and mysteries of nature, and hold its moments still just long enough for me to see reflections of my own heart and human condition. I find myself lingering in solidarity . . . pondering my own soul and the One who made all things.
—**Mark A. Looyenga**, D.Min., M.Div., M.S., Director of Soul Care, The Navigators

BELOW THE BRIGHTNESS

Steven Searcy

Scottsdale, Arizona • solumpress.com

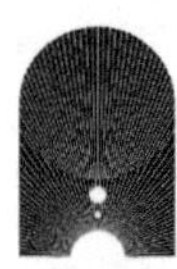

ISBN 979-8-9898558-0-3

Cover art and design by Sarah Christolini
Interior design by Riley Bounds and Sarah Christolini
Author photo by Peter Searcy

Library of Congress Cataloguing-in-Publication Data
Name: Searcy, Steven, author.
Title: Below the brightness / Steven Searcy.
Description: Scottsdale, AZ: Solum Literary Press, 2024.
Identifiers: LCCN 2024931403
ISBN: 979-8-9898558-0-3 (print)
ISBN: 979-8-9898558-1-0 (ePub)
Subjects: BISAC: POETRY / General / Subjects & Themes - Inspirational and Religious / American - General
LC record available at https://lccn.loc.gov/2024931403

To my grandfather, “Fafa,”
Karl G. Johnson Jr. (1934-2024),
who first encouraged me to love poetry,

and to my wife, Kaitlin,
who encourages me to receive the love of Jesus.

What is that which shines through me and strikes my heart without injury, making me tremble and kindling a fire in me? I shudder because I am unlike it, and yet I glow because I resemble it.

–Augustine of Hippo

Contents

Acknowledgments

Grateful acknowledgement is given to the editors of the following publications, where many of these poems first appeared (sometimes in earlier versions):

The North American Anglican: "Spark"
Ekstasis Magazine: "After Fall," "Tabernacle," "In the Shade of the Black Walnut"
Heart of Flesh Literary Journal: "Fly," "Following Vultures," "The Bread"
Pulsebeat Poetry Journal: "Long Winter," "Singing Lessons," "Moon," "Rise"
Reformed Journal: "Duplex: Lux," "Hush"
The Clayjar Review: "He Calls Them All By Name" (as "And can it be that he")
Solid Food Press: "The Pit"
UCity Review: "Marcescent," "Creek Walk"
Calla Press: "Safe," "The Large Oak"
Agape Review: "This Much I Know"
Foreshadow Magazine: "Misjudged," "Do What Cannot Be Left Undone," "Morning Prayer"
Commonweal Magazine: "Nativity Song"
Southern Poetry Review: "Listening"
Autumn Sky Poetry Daily: "Inside Voices"
Pure in Heart Stories: "Come Join the Song"
Sublunary Review: "To a Silent Pine"
Boats Against the Current: "Flycatcher"
Paddler Press: "Vernal"
Poems for Ephesians (McMaster Divinity College): "Ephesians 4:32"
Amethyst Review: "All Life Is Movement," "Dusk Fog"
The Windhover: "A Dream Is Just a Wish"
Fathom Magazine: "Summer Comes"

"A Little Thing" first appeared in *All Shall Be Well: An Anthology of New Poems for Julian of Norwich*, ed. Sarah Law (Amethyst Press, 2023).

The duplex form used in "Duplex: Lux" was originated by Jericho Brown. I would also like to thank Burl Horniachek for providing helpful feedback on an early version of the manuscript, and Riley Bounds and the team at Solum for making this book a reality.

BELOW THE BRIGHTNESS

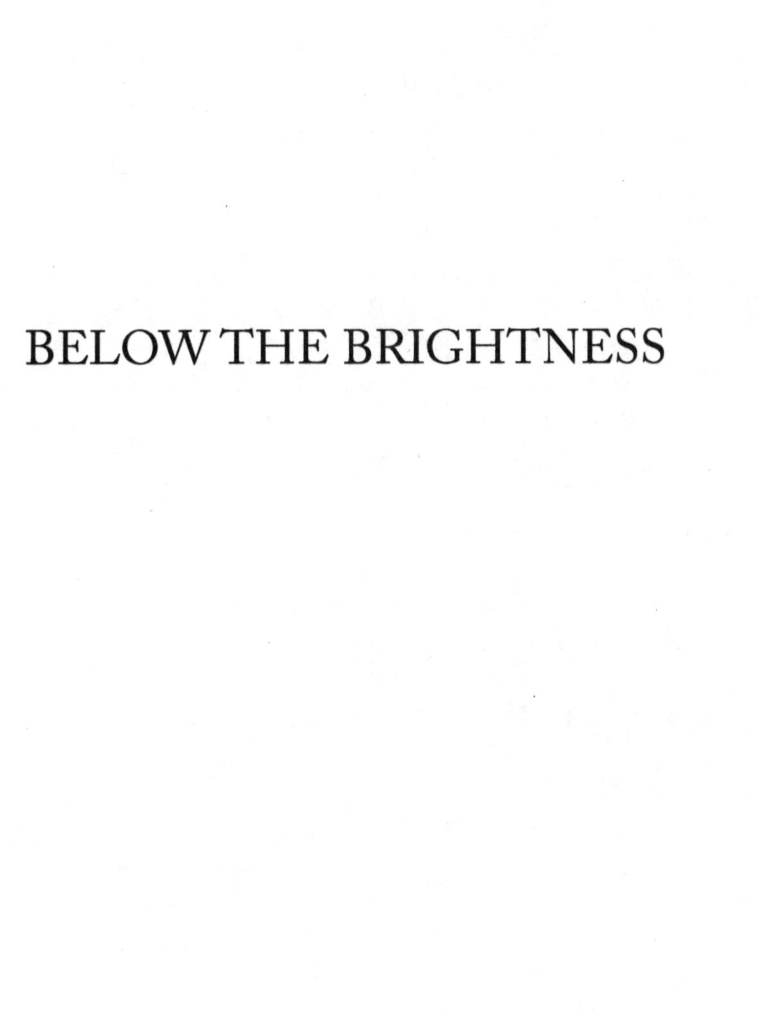

Spark

Glow, gentle canticle,
in the endless ether—
ring radiant across
the radius of curse—
flow faster than lashes,
ride with rigid grasp.

The hollows gape
and holler as you flash
in the shallows, a holy
sheen holding steady—
they didn't know about you
and the new brine we breathe.

Standing in the Wind

This autumn afternoon the wind is strong
and gentle, soft on shoulders in the sun,
chasing the withered loose leaves as they run,
speeding the scattered cotton clouds along.

In coruscating ripples on the lake's
bright top and in the canopy of green
and yellow is a force untamed, unseen
except through what it lifts and bends and shakes.

While standing here beneath the blue expanse,
my heart is stirred. I ask for nothing more:
          Lord, do not let me be a stone,
          still in the wind, unmoved, unblown,
                    but let me be
                    a hawk, a tree,
                              set free
                              to soar,
                              to dance.

After Fall

The world was gold—
it all fell down,
shriveled, turned brown,
speckled with mold.

The sky is clear,
but in each tree
and field, I see
predation, fear.

Each hungry eye
glances about
with the same shout—
I must not die!

All fingers strain,
grasping to stay
safe, to snatch prey,
to hold off pain.

Dry

Two crows
fly by.
I spy
the rows
of leaf-
less trees.
The breeze
breathes grief.

I touch
my head
and sigh.
So much
is dead
and dry.

Fly

That's me—that panicked fly
flailing against the bathroom window,
helplessly zizzing in a frantic attempt
to get back to where
I belong.

You would be happy
to help me get free—
you would scoop me into your hand
and fling me gently past all the screens and panes
into the fresh, open air,

if only I would stop
and let you catch me.

Unmooring

Of course my heart
is not adoring—
I'm much too busy poring
over every chart,
backing up, restoring
before things fall apart,
collecting, shoring
up my stock before the start
of winter, filling up my cart
before the floods come roaring—
I'm saving, storing
up treasure in the bank or smart
investments, while ignoring
the gentle voice
inviting me, imploring
me to make a different choice—
to take and taste—receive, rejoice.

Long Winter

The forests fade
and freeze, while fierce
winds whip and pierce,
and skies are greyed.

Each empty limb
no longer grieves
forgotten leaves.
The gaunt and grim

land shudders. All
that don't sleep fight
for life in white
wastes. Dense clouds crawl.

On a blank plain,
small hopes were carried
and lost—the buried
seeds still remain.

Following Vultures

I completed
the loop down the hill and
along the creek but

I could not find
what all the black vultures
are circling for.

And now I must
consider why I am not so
diligent to search

for the sick and
dying things in some corner
of my own chest.

In the Dark

Darkness. All around
is dark. The darkness sighs,
whispers, smothers cries.
No spark burns. There's no sound

but furtive wings and feet
that crave the dark's domain.
Even the bravest brain
still shivers in complete

darkness, as it clutches
shoulders and compresses
the chest. The dark undresses
the gorgeous and sordid. Much is

hidden and revealed
in darkness—watching, waiting,
forgetting, contemplating,
some things are lost, some healed.

Inside the unlit bowels
of the wood, one small beam
blooms like a languid dream,
floating over the howls

and holes, a thin wan glow—
of little use, but more
than dark, frosting the shore
of midnight's bleak tableau.

This pale and fickle ghost-
shine gleams because a bright
light burns beyond our sight—
the hope that we need most.

Duplex: Lux

Though you had always lived in light, you looked
deep in the dark, and chose the way of pain.

Deep in the dark, we chose the way of pain
and ran from the light in our fear and shame.

You ran from the light, into our fear and shame,
to where we sat soaked in well-deserved tears.

You wept a well of undeserved tears,
and limped with joy to the brutal cross.

We look with joy at the brutal cross, at
your pierced hands and outstretched arms, wide with love.

Your pierced hands and outstretched arms, wide with love,
reach to rescue us from our endless night.

You reached to rescue us from endless night,
and with you, we will always live in light.

He Calls Them All By Name

And can it be that he,
whose fingers molded mites
and crafted constellations,
who counts each mitochondrion
and rests upon the nebulae,

hangs upon my every word,
hears each heartbeat, sees each tear,
feels my sweat and pulse and breath,
and knows and knows and cares and cares?

The Pit

I am afraid
to even see
the tragedy—
the mess I've made.

Rage, greed, pride, doubt—
from my heart's store,
all these and more
come spewing out.

I am the pit
I'm in—dark, dank,
cold. Who can yank
me out of it?

One hand can plumb
these depths. When all
is lost, I call—
he said he'd come!

Marcescent

Mother Beech, who hugs the creek bank, teaches
a lesson to her scattered adolescent
children: she spends her winters nude, quiescent
through the constant chill. The smaller beeches
are resolute—although the weather bleaches
and withers, they won't accept the evanescent
nature of their leaves, till the incessant
press of wind in March finally breaches
their brutal grip, and paper leaves fly free.
Soon, slender buds will open in the pleasant
breeze of April, and the young will see
again the green unfurling, luminescent.
Next autumn, it's forgotten. Stubbornly,
they cling to what must fall away—marcescent.

Last

Last cen-
tury
this tree
was thin
and small,
now stand-
ing grand
and tall.

We hu-
mans grow
so fast,
but oh,
we do
not last.

Wary

I've failed
and failed and failed—
my soul's adept
at being assailed,
and won't accept
a thing, except
for being jailed
or self-impaled—

and yet, he wept—
he was nailed—

he died, revealing
the love that I've rejected—
he died, repealing
the charges I've collected—
and he was resurrected,
restoring and annealing
a heart so rusted and neglected,
a heart so thoroughly infected,
so desperately in need of healing—

he lavished me with love so undeserved I can't conceive it.
Let overwhelming love pervade me—help me to believe it!

Service

"How may I help you?" with a friendly zest
the boy behind the counter asks, his eyes
and ears attuned to my request, then flies
to satisfy my needs—I stand impressed.
And yet, why does he strive to do his best?
His paycheck, not my pleasure, is the prize.
Although he's kind, and fast to fetch my fries,
I am an obligation, not a guest.

With equal zeal a moral man may run
around, smiling and offering to lend
a helping hand, eager to do his part,
humming with restless effort—while the one
he serves is just a means to serve his end:
a merit badge to patch a loveless heart.

Safe

I lock the door,
engulfed in fear—
none can come near—
not anymore.

No need to weep.
No cause for bliss.
Secure in this
locked safe, I sleep.

Jesus, invade
my fortress. Break
my safe's lock. Make
me unafraid

of anything
but being far
from you—my star,
my rock, my king.

Tabernacle

So that our weak and wounded eyes could know
the brilliant beauty blazing bright above
and not be burned or blinded by that light
which shines unceasing, God decides to show
himself in part so we might glimpse his love
in full—a veil reveals him to our sight.

Wonderful cloaking! Words cannot convey
the way the incandescent image dims.
He stoops to wrap himself in rags of skin,
to coat his gorgeous gleam in cracking clay.
He hides his holy glow in humble limbs
and meekly mingles in the mess of men.

He drops into our darkened world to dwell,
covert in carnal camouflage. He bends
to enter earth so we can see and hear
his grace. He welcomes pain to make us well.
Enfolded in frail flesh, our Lord descends—
look, look at how our kind king Christ comes near!

This Much I Know

When grief and fears
make my tears flow,
this much I know—
my God has tears.

When I can't speak
or move at all,
this I recall—
my God was weak.

When searing shame
makes my wounds sting,
I know my king
has felt the same.

When I'm alone,
when all friends go,
this much I know—
that I am known.

Misjudged

Of course you will be
misunderstood.

Christ was a coward,
cold and uncaring,
reckless, foolish,
a loner, a lush,
arrogant, ill-tempered,
soft, and strange,
a troublemaker,
a small, stupid man,
a meaningless martyr.

What are you?

Nativity Song

What birthday could be stranger?
"Before Abraham was, I AM,"
born into mortal danger—
the wise man, shepherd, star, and lamb,
lying in a manger.

The scene is so absurd!
Bright troops announce the news with joy:
the first and final word
is born, a wordless baby boy—
the lowly ones have heard.

They leave their sheep behind
to see the king held by his mother.
Weak and nearly blind,
he comes to be our older brother—
to keep and seek and find.

This child is born to meet
us in our wandering—to be
the rock that's struck, the sweet
spring that flows, the mystery
of daily bread to eat.

He comes to be the snake
held up and stretched out on a rod,
to heal our wounds, to take
our curse—this little baby God,
breastfeeding, half awake.

He comes to bring a sword,
and to be pierced—to pay the wages
we could not afford.
Behold, the rocking rock of ages,
the shushed and swaddled Lord!

Listening

The shadows climb
over the ridge.
It's almost time.

Under the bridge,
a message from
the water's edge,

a throbbing drum
that asks and asks:
What will come?

The world of masks
and boxes churns
with countless tasks.

The moss and ferns
are meshed in prayer.
A song returns

to charm the air—
a clear, deep chime
that's hardly there.

Inside Voices

Along a bench, each nose is tipping up
or down, each eye is wide or almost shut,
some lips are pursed, some suck a coffee cup,
and some might even smile a moment. But

inside each face's scowl or vacant stare,
there is a toddler singing just for joy—
unfettered, fervent, wholly unaware
of judgment or position. Is a boy

or girl the first thing that you notice when
you look in someone's eyes? And are their squeals
of glee in your ears? Stop and look again—
think how the tread is worn on years-old wheels—

they're there, somehow, somewhere, inside, beneath
the shards of broken glass and shells embossed
with rust, behind the shining, lying teeth.
Why shouldn't every precious child be lost?

The hands that hold at first are generally
gone at some point, in some way, and cruel
or empty words are flung. Someone's a bully.
Someone serves you tea, or scoops your gruel.

And always there are thunderstorms, and huge
oaks come crashing down. How do we ever
manage to stand here in this centrifuge,
where silent scissors loom, waiting to sever

the plainest, finest things—paper balloons
and china dolls and ink pen doodles? If only
we could hear those open, glowing tunes
bursting from tiny throats, now bent and lonely.

How would you look at someone if you heard
their oldest melody or glimpsed the wings
they wore before they ceased to be a bird,
before they settled into saner things?

Do What Cannot Be Left Undone

Do what cannot be left undone—
before the chiming clock,
before the rising sun,
before the sky turns black,
before the war is won,
do what cannot be left undone.

Say what cannot be left unsaid—
before the doorbell rings,
before the daily bread,
before the sparrow sings,
before the sun turns red,
say what cannot be left unsaid.

Do what cannot be left undone—
before the mountains fall,
before the rivers run,
before the crickets call,
before the yarn is spun,
do what cannot be left undone.

Say what cannot be left unsaid—
before the frigid night,
before the books are read,
before the dimming light,
before the empty bed,
say what cannot be left unsaid.

Come Join the Song

Come join the song—sing praises loud and plain
to Christ the Lamb, who lives though he was slain.
He took the whip, spit, thorns, nails, jeers, disdain,
and utter isolation in his pain,
then dropped into the grave—but not in vain!
By death, he transformed loss into great gain—
what once was Satan's boon became his bane.
Christ chose to die, to conquer death's domain.
Our Jesus has destroyed death's lock and chain,
and rises to his throne where he will reign
for good. No fear and sadness will remain,
and all his children join to sing the loud refrain.

Singing Lessons

How do you teach
a child to sing? You sing to them.
Sing sweetly, freely, each
and every night,
along with dim
moonlight.

Sing sun,
on open paths
where rivers run,
for wings aloft.
For clouds and puddle baths,
sing soft.

Again,
how do you teach a child to sing?
You sing. Keep singing when
it's all that you can do.
Sing anything.
Keep singing. You.

The Whisper

The surveyor's tripod stands there on the ground
as I pass by, and I'm surprised to hear
an urgent voice whispering in my ear:
Quick—knock it down, while no one is around—
you won't be back this way—you won't be found—
think how mysterious it will appear—
a bit of silly fun, nothing severe—
just some small equipment, abruptly downed.

Lucky, I passed on and escaped the spell—
but how could such a violent voice seem sweet
and tame in justifying raising hell?
Snaking around for someone else to meet,
the same wild whisper nudged a storm to fell
an oak tree on a house just down the street.

To a Silent Pine

O pine, silent, lichen-crusted,
standing by Johnson Ferry Road,
do you hear the snarling engines
and smell the pumping gasoline?

Does your west side, bereft of limbs,
still feel where those branches once hung
gathering afternoon sunrays
before they were amputated?

Do your roots remember ground
before the conduits snaked through?
Do your fingers remember air
before the cell antennas rose?

Shaped by upheaval yet unmoved,
letting the interlopers pass,
your cracked and mottled trunk stood here
before it became a by-way.

Invasive

A spreading clump of knotweed shivers in
the wind. The sky grows greyer as the storm
approaches. Brittle vines and privet crowd
around the nearly horizontal elms
that stretch across the creek. Beneath, a caved-
in bank with layers of sediment exposed.
Chunks of glass are mingled in the stones.
Another chilly gust. Stray petals rain.
The hardwoods wearing English ivy cloaks
clutch them closer. Time to head back home.

Fruitless

My heart makes one
sweet promise, then
another. When
will I be done

with promising
beyond what I
can manage? My
pale offering

is nothing more
than words. I do
not follow through.
I'm waging war

against the me
I wish I was.
I flail, because
I am not free.

Flycatcher

It's warm for early March,
and the phoebes are feasting
on flies too small to be seen
unless backlit by the soft sun
streaming through the branches
that are still mostly empty
but will soon be unfolding
with a grandeur unmatched
by the staggering boasts of men
who think they can tame the sky,
or build something that will last,
or catch a fly.

Branch

Air warms.
Sap swells.
New cells.
Wild storms.
Swift wind.
Hang tight.
Drink light.
Extend.

Bloom late,
bloom long.

Bear weight,
grow strong.

Slow wait,
sweet song.

Vernal

A million medallions emerge,
and marriage beds spread everywhere,
and everywhere sparkles and flushes
with color, and clear air hums
some tongueless song, a long tone,
a lingering tune, even stones
are singing green, greeting warm,
and storms just juice the growth,
as each leaf lifts to light.

Someplace

Suburban street, curved curb, slim house with vinyl
siding—in back, a chewed-through, leaning fence—
behind, a strip of wild—the creek, where once
we saw a mink, banks thick with brush. Infernal
mosquitoes roil for seven months or more.
Four years ago the county bulldozed through
and left a concrete dome and laid new sewer
pipes. Why should anybody know or care?

This is a place, this wisp of world, a home—
where possums tramp through moonglow, spider silk
stretches from hickory to baby beech,
whose mother reaches from the creekside loam,
and silverbell and sourwood offer each
beleaguered bee sweet bowls of mercy-milk.

Morning Prayer

When morning sunshine streams between green leaves
and the breeze blows but there are no clouds to drift,
let me receive the gift—
let my heart hymn,
and as my soul receives,
let me remember where the world is dim.

When callow clouds camp out and gray the earth
and the weight of shadows presses hope slim, let
me see what's not here yet—
let my heart trust
that there will be new birth
one day, that life can be remade from dust.

Ephesians 4:32

Be kind as springtime sun to slender shoots,
as kind as April rain to stretching roots.
Be tender as a mother robin on
her nest, as tender as the dew at dawn,
as dogwood petals starting to unfold.

But how can we be kind when hearts are cold
and shriveled? How can we be tender when
we're filled with thorns and brittle stems, so thin
and barren that it seems nothing could save us?
He forgave us. He forgave us. He forgave us.

In the Branches

Climb in the branches, sweet child, on a day
in spring, when the air is abundantly clear.
Take chances, and hoist yourself up through the green
to the blue—be alive, rife with breath, full of play.
From this pinnacle perching-point, everything's near,
everything's wonderful, everything's seen,

up in the branches where mockingbirds preen.
Balancing perfectly, high without fear,
in a flickering freedom that won't fly away,
alert and aloft, be astounded, between
the beauty that's here and that isn't yet here,
even as breezes cause branches to sway.

Giver

Giver of every gulp,
of every good grin,
giver of green, of growth,
of gulls and gills,
gazelles and grapes,
great giver, mind-boggling,
prodigal, gleaming—
we glean a glimpse
of your grace and we guffaw,
gladly. You grant, and give,
and then you give and give still—
even to greedy grinches,
even to ungrateful grumps.
Good giver, golden,
gorgeous—your glory glows,
great God, and all good gifts
gush to us from you.

All Life Is Movement

The obvious mockingbirds,   the subtle pines
standing, expanding,   earthworms wending through
warm humus,   soft moss pillows blooming,   vines
stalking, winding,   dark swallows dashing to
the treetops,   algae pluming in the pond,
a spinning spider and a ceaseless fly,
stone-still coral,   an unfurling fern frond,
a distant osprey flashing in the sky—
the outer parts or the innermost are al-
ways circulating, working, flitting, fill-
ing, extending,   quick or slow,   large or small,
each in its own way dancing,   never still—
everything living moves and weaves and strives
because love moves, and the Lord of love lives.

The Music of the World

The music of the world is wound
around each leaping molecule—
in alpine air and underground
the music of the world is wound—
a drastic dance, a raucous sound
that stirs and steers, a vital fuel—
the music of the world is wound
around each leaping molecule.

A Little Thing

"...he showed me a little thing, the quantity of a hazelnut, in the palm of my hand..."
–Julian of Norwich

A simple psalm,
pleasant and terse:
the universe,
cupped in a palm.

All things are his—
the Lord of glory,
who speaks the story
of all that is.

But when we glimpse that marble in his hands,
we crave the gleaming speck of beauty, losing
sight of the sturdy, ageless arms, refusing
the maker as the universe expands—

though sprawling mountain peaks and spinning galaxies
seem huge to us, and heaps of gold and diamonds glow,
it's all too small to fill our hearts. All good things flow
from him, the only good. He holds it all. He sees

our need and offers us himself—he gives us everything.
And yet, we're restless folks—legs ache, necks twist, and eyes
won't shut—
why do we try to sleep scrunched up inside a hazelnut,
when every single night we could be resting in a king?

Hush

Much noise surrounds.
Let words be few.
Sit. Listen. Chew.
Then hear the sounds

of trees and birds.
Sit. Breathe. Release.
And taste the peace
too deep for words.

There is no fire.
Stop the alarms.
You're held by arms
that cannot tire.

Wings

A little wren can lift itself—a push,
a flap, a flash—it's gone from ground to bush
or branch. Some days I wish that I could lift
myself so easily—but what a gift
instead, that I can make a needy cry
and speedy wings swoop down to lift me high.

Soil Horizon

The flowers brim with color, speaking grace
and hope to battered hearts, a living feast
for humming things, the boldest spark of life—
surrounded by the shine of green, upheld
by stalks and stems, and fed by roots that weave
within the earth. The flowers always come
with joy and always go—they fade and wither.
Leaves and petals fall when called—diving
downward to be mulched into nutritious
nothingness. Beneath each flashing flower,
generations of crumbling cellulose
releasing nitrogen and phosphorus,
nourishing fresh blooms. How natural
for human hearts to seek the flower's glory,
the blossoming of beauty, new and vivid,
noticed and loved—but who will be the soil?

Creek Walk

Why are you always wading in the creek?
What do you crave? What secrets do you seek?
The swerving roots exposed by rushing flow
are tracing out your curving route. Go slow
and listen to their hints. The sunlight glints
on quaking pools. Your stepping makes no sense
to anyone, and even you're unsure
how long this restless question can endure
and where this way will lead. Why do you need
to wade this way? Today this playful deed
becomes a somber ritual—a dance
of urgent trepidation. Just a glancc
toward home, then onward, onward—don't delay.
You do not need your eyes. You know the way—
the swirl, the gush will push you on—the tickle
twists and thrills you. All the faint and fickle
advertisements filling up your screens
are nothing now. You don't know what it means,
but something chattering around you makes
a sound that breaks your barrier. It takes
a while, but then you hear—you've heard it often
but forgotten it again. You soften—
you blend into the rivulets that wend
their way through stone and silt, around each bend,
coursing on and on—whirls without end.

A Distant Shore

Although I haven't been there yet,
I've heard there is a distant shore
with no disease, no threat of war,
and no more longing or regret.

I've heard there is no theft or debt,
no counting down or keeping score,
although I haven't been there yet.
I've heard there is a distant shore

where cheeks are never cold or wet,
where backs don't ache and hearts aren't sore—
a tranquil coast where storms don't roar
and there's no sun to rise or set.
Although I haven't been there yet,
I've heard there is a distant shore.

A Dream Is Just a Wish

A dream is just a wish—
hope is something more:
a whiff of something fresh,

a glimpse of open door,
the faintest strain of far-
off strings, a drifting spore,

a filled and sealed-up jar
resting in a cellar,
a secret reservoir,

an engine, a propeller,
a cannon of confetti,
a shining rim, a stellar

wind, a ship that's ready.
A dream is just a wish—
hope is something steady.

Moon

This night
in June,
the moon
is quite

a bright
balloon,
but soon
the light

of day
will banish
her beams

and they
will vanish
like dreams.

Rise

Out on
a limb
at dawn,
a hymn.

Clouds yawn,
wake up,
and don
make-up.

Mist grips
the hill.
Dew drips.
All still.

Day breaks—
heart quakes.

The Large Oak

Just off the hilltop's crest he stands,
reaching up and down. In rain
he does not cower or complain,
but waits, receives with open hands.
He does not run or make demands.
In wind he laughs and sways. In sun
he sings. His work is never done.
Ever at rest, he folds his hands
and lifts a solemn word of praise
each of his hundred thousand days.

The Bread

The bread is always on the table,
always fresh, always within reach.

But we pound our fists, petulant,
demanding something different.
We scowl and pout.

Or worse, we fold our hands and lie
that we aren't hungry,
that we don't want anything, smiling
to silence the incessant gnawing in our guts.

In the Shade of the Black Walnut

That which must heal you
also may harm you.

Renewal only comes
from surrender to a hand
that is powerful
and unpredictable
and good
and unsafe.

You must sit in an open field,
far enough from any shelter
that you may be overtaken
when lightning strikes.

To taste a fresh egg
you must expose yourself to snakes.

To exist alone
is to be barely alive.
In order to be full of life
you must teem with the life
of all the world's beings.

You must share the grass
in bare feet, with the dogs
and ants and things
too small to be seen.
Every arachnid must be
your neighbor for that glorious hour

on the hilltop in the shade
of the black walnut tree.

Learn to let the ants share
your skin. Let your skin become
part of the hill, as it once was.
Let your heart become a landing strip
for any winged thing that might fly near.

Your skin is always
harboring something,
or it is disappearing.
So set it free,
to be handled by hands
that you do not understand.

Summer Comes

Already sweetgum balls are dangling green
and there's no longer any need for pants.
I hear a blue jay scream. Dragonflies dance
wildly, while clouds drift careless and serene.

This seems surreal when so much time is spent
in fighting not to shiver, using up
meager reserves, scraping an empty cup.
Our bones know lack. Emptiness won't relent.

Yet somehow summer always comes, to teach
our bodies about abundance, to show
us shocking growth, to feather us in shade,
to feed us with every color. Below
the brightness we see so much newness made.
A time will come for basking on the beach.

Dusk Fog

As pastel clouds bloom, stretch, and slack,
mist rises from the hillside's back.
Dishes get washed. The kids get hugs
and story time. The lightning bugs
and bats show up to flash and flit.
The treetop's now a silhouette
in the fading light. All the day's rough
words and anxious thoughts are enough
to bleach the evening's beauty, when
they're fully felt. The softness in
the warm air whispers wordlessly
that maybe wrecked hearts can still be
restored, as this simple, lonely place
awaits the night, shrouded in grace.

About the Author

Steven Searcy grew up in Huntsville, Alabama, and received degrees from Vanderbilt University and Georgia Institute of Technology. He currently lives with his wife and four sons in Atlanta, Georgia, where he works as an engineer in the field of fiber optic telecommunications. This is his first book.

www.ingramcontent.com/pod-product-compliance
Lightning Source LLC
LaVergne TN
LVHW090536110826
845146LV00003B/1123

* 9 7 9 8 9 8 9 8 5 5 8 0 3 *